KU-759-451

PUFFIN BOOKS

UK | USA | Canada | Ireland | Australia
India | New Zealand | South Africa

Puffin Books is part of the Penguin Random House group of companies
whose addresses can be found at global.penguinrandomhouse.com.

www.penguin.co.uk
www.puffin.co.uk
www.ladybird.co.uk

First published 2016
001

Written by Daniel Roy

Printed in Slovakia

A CIP catalogue record for this book is available from the British Library

ISBN: 978–0–141–36991–4

All correspondence to:
Puffin Books
Penguin Random House Children's
80 Strand, London WC2R 0RL

EXPLORATION
AND ADVENTURE
HANDBOOK

PUFFIN

INTRODUCTION

IT'S A BIG, BEAUTIFUL WORLD OUT THERE. LET'S GO CHECK IT OUT!

Hello there, business partner! I'm the Traveling Merchant. One of my clients, the Guide, asked me to give you a guided tour of Terraria – in exchange for a small fee, of course. All I ask in return is that you consider some of my fine wares next time I'm in town. Think of it as a mutually beneficial partnership!

From the depths of the Underworld to Floating Islands in the sky and everything in-between, I'll take you on an adventure through all the wonders and perils that Terraria has to offer.

Just try to stay alive, all right? I don't need a second Skeleton Merchant cornering my mobile merchandise business!

BEGINNER TIP

New to Terraria? Look for *Terraria: The Ultimate Survival Handbook* at your local bookshop or online retailer! Future master builders may also enjoy *Terraria: Crafting and Construction Handbook*.

CONTENTS

Once in a while a friendly face will chime in with helpful advice. I even got the Angler to write an entire guide on fishing. You can imagine how much that cost me!

CHAPTER ONE: THE WORLD AT A GLANCE

Each world you create in Terraria is unique, but they have a few things in common.

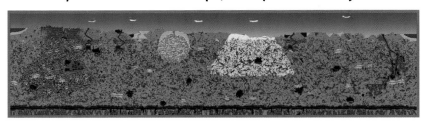

BIOMES

Each and every world in Terraria is made up of distinct environments called **biomes**. Each world features the Forest, Snow, Desert and Jungle biomes, with an Ocean biome at either end of the world.

Every world also features an **evil biome**: either the Crimson or the Corruption, but never both. You'll also find the **Dungeon** somewhere near the Ocean on the opposite side to the Jungle.

LAYERS

Just like a delicious birthday cake, your world is also made up of **layers**. From top to bottom, they are: Space, Surface, Underground, Cavern and Underworld. You'll spend most of your time either on the surface, or below ground in the Underground and Cavern layers.

NIGHT AND DAY

Your world goes through a whole day in twenty-four minutes of real time. Night starts at 7:30 p.m., at which point **zombies** and **Demon Eyes** will start to appear. It's better to stay indoors or seek shelter underground at first, at least until you can find or craft better gear.

The sun rises at 4:30 a.m., when the zombies will quietly return to wherever they came from.

BEGINNER TIP

You can learn all about surviving your first night in **Chapter Three: The First Day** on page 21 of *The Ultimate Survival Handbook.*

TELLING THE TIME

To ensure you make it home before the Zombie Apocalypse, consider carrying a watch in your inventory. You can craft all watches by placing a **table** and **chair** together and using them as a crafting station.

WATCH TYPE	INGREDIENTS	PRECISION
Copper	Copper Bar (10), Chain (1)	To the hour
Tin	Tin Bar (10), Chain (1)	
Silver	Silver (10), Chain (1)	To the half-hour
Tungsten	Tungsten (10), Chain (1)	
Gold	Gold (10), Chain (1)	To the minute
Platinum	Platinum (10), Chain (1)	

EXPLORATION ORDER

Terraria is a wide, open world that you can explore in whatever order you want. That said, if you get stuck or find enemies too difficult, just refer to this quick step-by-step guide for tips as to where you should go next. If you make sure you have all the tools, weapons and armour corresponding to a given step before you move on, it'll make things a lot easier!

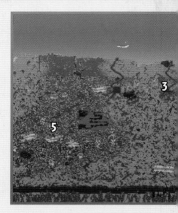

1. EXPLORE THE FOREST, SNOW AND DESERT

Stay close to the surface for your first expeditions, but be sure to check out any cave you come across. Pots and chests contain valuable treasure that will help you on your quest! Aim to make it home each day before nightfall.

2. HEAD UNDERGROUND

At this point, some brave adventurers make a push through the Corruption or Crimson to reach the Ocean and pick up the Angler . . . but that's up to you. Why not make your way to the Underground and Cavern layers instead, gathering as much ore and treasure as you can? Be particularly careful if you run across special biomes such as the Marble Cave, as the monsters that roam there could be too tough for you to beat at this point in the game.

3. DEFEAT THE CORRUPTION OR THE CRIMSON

Getting comfortable underground? Have you defeated the Eye of Cthulhu? You might be ready to face the Corruption or the Crimson and all that those biomes can throw at you. Destroy some Shadow Orbs or Crimson Hearts, and try your luck with the evil boss lurking there.

4. MASTER THE DUNGEON

Once the Corruption or Crimson has yielded all you need, it's time to face Skeletron and enter the Dungeon! Once inside, look out for Golden Chests containing extra-awesome weapons and items.

5. SURVEY THE UNDERGROUND JUNGLE

The Underground Jungle offers some of the biggest challenges in the game. Head there when you're ready for an adventure. Make sure you check out the Bee Hives along the way and try your luck beating Queen Bee! See the Bee Hive section on page 40 for details.

6. DIG DOWN TO THE UNDERWORLD

It's time for the ultimate challenge! Head to the Underworld and carefully mine Hellstone and Obsidian. Craft yourself a set of **Molten Armor** and start preparing to unlock Hardmode!

CHAPTER TWO: BIOMES

Welcome to Terraria! Pretty, isn't it? I should start charging admission!

THE FOREST

Almost all adventurers start their career in the Forest – although a few begin in the Snow instead. It's safe to explore during the day, but ... Well, you already know what happens at nightfall.

MONSTER SPOTTERS' GUIDE

MONSTER	NOTES
Green Slime	
Blue Slime	Drop Gel
Purple Slime	
Pinky (rare)	Drops Pink Gel and a Gold Coin.
Goblin Scout (rare)*	Drops Tattered Cloth
King Slime (rare)*	Boss
Umbrella Slime**	Sometimes drops Umbrella Hat
Flying Fish**	Drops 90 Copper Coins

* Appears only in the outer two thirds of the map.
** During rain only

NATURAL RESOURCES

Wood

Mushroom

Sunflower

Daybloom

Yellow Marigold

Blue Berries

Copper Ore

Tin Ore

Iron Ore

Lead Ore

Pumpkin
(Halloween only)

FISHING GUIDE

Bass

Salmon

Balloon Pufferfish

Bomb Fish

Frog Leg

Zephyr Fish

Wooden Crate

Iron Crate

Golden Crate

UNIQUE SIGHTS

CAVE EXPEDITIONS

The Forest features many cave entrances leading underground. Be sure to check them out for **pots** and **chests** containing helpful loot! These chests contain many useful items including ore, arrows, potions, rope and torches, as well as rarer items such as the **Aglet**, **Climbing Claws**, the **radar** and the **Wand of Sparking**.

Aaaw ...

THE CUTEST SLIME

A rare Slime called **Pinky** sometimes wanders the Forest. Although tougher than other Slimes, it drops **Pink Gel**, which you can use to craft lots of unique bouncy items. Beating Pinky will also get you 1 Gold coin!

SHINY CRITTERS

Gold versions of normal critters will sometimes appear in the Forest. Grab a **bug net** from the Merchant for 25 Silver and use it to catch them. You can sell them back for 10 Gold each!

Come on! Jump in my wallet, little guy!

Like a slimier version of 'Ride of the Valkyries'

IT'S RAINING SLIME!

Slime is so prevalent in Terraria that it will sometimes fall from the sky! Beat 150 Slimes and the **Slime King** will appear.

THE UNDERGROUND

Head below ground and you'll eventually run into the **Underground layer**. Monsters here are more aggressive than on the surface, but the ore and treasures you'll find will be worth your while. You should always have a stock of **torches, ropes** and **Wooden Platforms** to get you through the twists and turns of the Underground.

MONSTER SPOTTERS' GUIDE

MONSTER	NOTES
Giant Worm	Sometimes drops whoopie cushion
Blue Slime	Drops gel
Red Slime	More powerful than Blue Slime, drops gel
Yellow Slime	
Pinky (rare)	Drops Pink Gel and a Gold Coin
Blue Jellyfish	Drops glowsticks, and sometimes drops Jellyfish Necklace
Piranha	Can drop hook, Robot Hat or compass

NATURAL RESOURCES

Glowing Mushroom

Blinkroot

Copper Ore

Tin Ore

Iron Ore

Lead Ore

Silver Ore

Tungsten Ore

Gold Ore

Platinum Ore

Demonite Ore (rare)

Crimtane Ore (rare)

Gems

Life Crystal

FISHING GUIDE

Armored Cavefish

Bass

Golden Carp

Specular Fish (Under Forest)

Stinkfish

Balloon Pufferfish

Bomb Fish

Frog Leg

Rockfish

Zephyr Fish

Wooden Crate

Iron Crate

Golden Crate

UNIQUE SIGHTS

THE COMPETITION

Down underground there's a despicable fellow called the **Skeleton Merchant**. This dishonest competitor is trying to put me out of business, by cutting on operational costs such as food or skincare products. If you really must go to him, he'll sell you items such as **Lesser Healing Potions**, **rope** and **torches**. Check out his stock at different times of the day and at various phases of the moon for some extra gear. This includes **counterweights** for your yo-yos, as well as **Spelunker Glowsticks** and the **Magic Lantern** – two items that make nearby treasure glow.

MY HEART WILL GO ON

As you explore the Underground and Cavern layers, you'll come across **Crystal Hearts**. Smash one with a pickaxe and you'll get a **Life Crystal**, which you can use to add 20 to your maximum Health. You can raise your Health to a maximum of 400 this way, at which point you can use Life Crystals to craft **Heart Lanterns** instead, which increase your life regeneration when placed. Or better yet, sell them to me. I'll give you a fair price!

ANYBODY HOME?

Wander long enough down below and you'll run into **underground cabins** filled with furniture, pots and even the occasional chest and statue. Chests, especially **Golden Chests**, are a source of highly valuable treasure such as the **Cloud in a Bottle** or the **Magic Mirror**, so make a habit of checking them out!

THE CAVERNS

Dig deeper still and you'll eventually hit the Cavern layer. The bottom of the Cavern is filled with lava pools, so tread carefully! In this layer, you'll also find the Cavern extensions of some of the surface biomes: the **Underground Snow, Underground Desert** and **Underground Jungle**.

MONSTER SPOTTERS' GUIDE

MONSTER	NOTES
Giant Worm	Sometimes drops whoopie cushion
Black Slime	Can inflict Darkness debuff
Mother Slime	Splits into Baby Slimes on death, sometimes drops compass
Skeleton	Sometimes drops hook or other items
Undead Miner	Can drop hook, mining equipment or other items
Cave Bat	Sometimes drops chain knife or depth meter
Salamander	Can drop depth meter, compass or Rally
Cochineal Beetle	Drops Red Husk (dye ingredient)
Pinky (rare)	Drops Pink Gel and a Gold Coin
Tim (rare)	Drops Wizard Hat
Nymph (rare)	Disguised as Lost Girl; often drops metal detector
Blue Jellyfish	Drops glowsticks, and sometimes drops Jellyfish Necklace
Piranha	Can drop hook, Robot Hat or compass
Giant Shelly	Sometimes drop depth meter, compass or Rally
Crawdad	

NATURAL RESOURCES

Glowing Mushroom   Blinkroot   Iron Ore   Lead Ore   Silver Ore   Tungsten Ore   Gold Ore

Platinum Ore   Demonite Ore (rare)   Crimtane Ore (rare)   Obsidian   Gems   Life Crystal   Copper Ore

FISHING GUIDE

Armored
Cavefish

Bass

Blue Jellyfish

Golden Carp

Specular Fish

Stinkfish

Balloon
Pufferfish

Bomb Fish

Frog Leg

Rockfish

Zephyr Fish

Wooden Crate

Iron Crate

Golden Crate

UNIQUE SIGHTS

YOUR LUCKY DAY

Though they're quite rare, you might encounter a **Gemstone Cave** filled to the brink with precious gems. These caves contain one type - or sometimes two types - of gems, which you can tell by the colour of the walls.

A Topaz Gemstone Cave

SOME CALL HIM TIM

Fancy a **Wizard Hat**? Take out the mean-spirited skeleton called Tim and he'll drop one. Just watch out: his magic attacks can hit you even through blocks.

Tim launching attacks through blocks

HEY THERE, LITTLE G—AAAAHH!!!

Don't trust anything you encounter deep below, even if it's a **Lost Girl**. This innocent-looking damsel is just waiting for you to get close enough before she turns into a **nymph** and beats the snot out of you! Kill her and you might get a **metal detector** for your troubles: this item will display the names of precious metals nearby.

Chivalry's about to get killed.

SNOW

The Snow biome is just like the Forest, except frozen. Around these parts, even the zombies wrap up warm. It's rare, but on occasion you'll begin in this environment when you enter a new world.

MONSTER SPOTTERS' GUIDE

MONSTER	NOTES
Ice Slime	Attacks reduce movement speed

NATURAL RESOURCES

Boreal Wood   Shiverthorn   Copper Ore   Tin Ore   Iron Ore   Lead Ore

FISHING GUIDE

Atlantic Cod   Bass   Frost Minnow   Balloon Pufferfish   Bomb Fish   Frog Leg   Frost Daggerfish

Zephyr Fish   Wood Crate   Iron Crate   Golden Crate

HAPPY FEET

The Snow biome doesn't have squirrels and bunnies ... but it has penguins! There's not much to do with these critters besides putting them in a terrarium to create a Penguin in a Cage. If you really like penguins, search deep underground for a fish, which will let you summon your own baby penguin pet. Flip to the **Underground Snow** section for more details!

16

DRESSING FOR THE WEATHER

The zombies you'll meet in the Snow biome know how to stay warm. So can you! Although this is pretty rare, the **Zombie Eskimos** will sometimes drop the **Eskimo Hood**, **Coat** and **Pants**. This cosy clothing won't give much of a boost to your stats, but at least you won't look like you're about to freeze to death.

M-mind if I borrow that c-c-coat?

Mmm . . . Marshmallows . . .

YUMMY!

If you build a house in the Snow biome and have the **Merchant** move in, he will sell you **marshmallows** for 1 Silver apiece. You can combine them with Wood to create **Marshmallow on a Stick**. Hold this over a campfire for ten seconds and it will turn into a **Cooked Marshmallow**, which will give you a boost to your combat stats when eaten.

RECIPE	INGREDIENTS	CRAFTING STATION
Marshmallow on a Stick (1)	Wood (1) Marshmallow (1)	By Hand

ICE ICE BABY

You can sometimes find **Ice Chests** in the Snow biome's caves. These contain a number of unique and very useful items such as ice skates, Snowball Cannon, Blizzard in a Bottle and Flurry Boots, as well as the Ice Boomerang and the powerful Ice Blade, which shoots frozen bolts at enemies. Can't find an Ice Chest? Head down to the **Underground Snow** . . . Turn the page for the lowdown!

UNDERGROUND SNOW

If you're worried about overheating from the lava, don't worry: there's still plenty of opportunity to cool down around here. The surface's Snow environment extends all the way down into the Cavern layer.

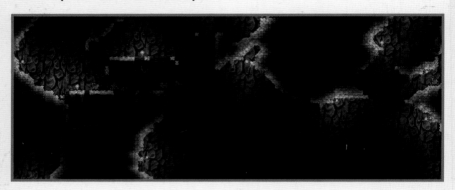

MONSTER SPOTTERS' GUIDE

MONSTER	NOTES
Ice Slime	Same as surface Slimes
Spiked Ice Slime	Shoots icicles, attacks can slow down or freeze in place
Ice Bat	Sometimes drops depth meter
Snow Flinx	Can drop compass or Snowball Launcher
Undead Viking	Can drop hook, compass or Viking Helmet
Cyan Beetle	Drops Cyan Husk (dye ingredient)

NATURAL RESOURCES

Shiverthorn   Iron Ore   Lead Ore   Silver Ore   Tungsten Ore   Gold Ore   Platinum Ore

Demonite Ore (rare)   Crimtane Ore (rare)   Gems   Life Crystal   Copper Ore   Tin Ore

FISHING GUIDE

 Armored Cavefish

 Atlantic Cod

 Bass

 Blue Jellyfish

 Frost Minnow

 Golden Carp

 Stinkfish

 Balloon Pufferfish

 Bomb Fish

 Frog Leg

 Frost Daggerfish

 Rockfish

 Zephyr Fish

 Wooden Crate

 Iron Crate

 Golden Crate

UNIQUE SIGHTS

FROZEN TREASURE

The Underground Snow and Upper Snow are the only biomes where you'll find **Ice Chests**, which contain some unique and useful treasure. Loot them for a chance to find the Ice Boomerang, Ice Blade, ice skates, Snowball Cannon, Blizzard in a Bottle or Flurry Boots. If you're lucky, you might even find the fish that will let you summon your own **baby penguin**!

BY ODIN'S BEARD!

You know what's worse than a skeleton? A loud, violent, frozen skeleton. Every time

DESERT

Sand: it's coarse, rough and it gets everywhere. But it's also useful for making glass, and cactus grows on it, so there are plenty of reasons to explore the Desert biome. Once you enter Hardmode, the Desert is especially vulnerable to the Corruption, the Crimson or the Hallow, so go see it while it lasts!

MONSTER SPOTTERS' GUIDE

MONSTER	NOTES
Sand Slime	Similar to regular Slimes
Antlion	
Antlion Swarmer	Drop Antlion Mandible
Antlion Charger	
Vulture	Flying monster
Blue Jellyfish	Drops glowsticks, and sometimes drops Jellyfish Necklace
Piranha	Can drop hook, Robot Hat or compass

NATURAL RESOURCES

Cactus | Waterleaf | Pink Prickly Pear | Copper Ore | Tin Ore | Iron Ore | Lead Ore

FISHING GUIDE

Bass | Balloon Pufferfish | Bomb Fish | Frog Leg | Zephyr Fish | Wooden Crate | Iron Crate

Gold Crate

UNIQUE SIGHTS

PYRAMID SCHEME

Some worlds feature a buried **pyramid** that you can access from the surface. If yours does, you're in luck; the pyramid contains a treasure room with pots, coin stashes and unique loot like the flying carpet, Sandstorm in a Bottle, Pharaoh's Mask and Pharaoh's Robe.

Time for some tomb raiding!

Day five: the cacti still think I'm one of them.

CACTUS MAN

One great reason to head to the Desert early is to collect **cactus**. Chop down those cacti and use them to craft yourself everything from armour to a funky green pickaxe! You can even craft furniture like the Cactus Chair . . . although why someone would want to sit on that is anyone's guess.

WATCH YOUR STEP

One of the Desert biomes in your world will feature a deep pit that leads down to a network of tunnels below the surface. With a little digging you can even reach the Underground Desert through there. It's a lot of fun to explore the Antlion-infested warrens, but be sure to bring **rope** so you can lower yourself safely down to the bottom of the pit.

UNDERGROUND DESERT

See that deep chasm leading to a labyrinth of tunnels under your Desert? It's one of the largest environments in the whole game. It's not for the faint of heart either: I'd advise holding off from exploring the Underground Desert until you have **Silver** or **Tungsten Armor**.

MONSTER SPOTTERS' GUIDE

MONSTER	NOTES
Antlion	
Antlion Swarmer	Drop Antlion Mandible
Antlion Charger	
Tomb Crawler	Can attack through walls

NATURAL RESOURCES

 Desert Fossil

 Waterleaf

 Iron Ore

 Lead Ore

 Silver Ore

 Tungsten Ore

 Gold Ore

 Platinum Ore

 Demonite Ore (rare)

 Crimtane Ore (rare)

 Gems

 Life Crystal

 Copper Ore

 Tin Ore

FISHING GUIDE

 Armored Cavefish

 Bass

 Blue Jellyfish

 Golden Carp

 Stinkfish

 Balloon Pufferfish

 Bomb Fish

 Frog Leg

 Rockfish

 Zephyr Fish

 Wooden Crate

 Iron Crate

 Golden Crate

UNIQUE SIGHTS

JURASSIC PERKS

The Underground Desert is the only place you can find **Desert Fossil**. By using it on an **Extractinator**, you can turn Desert Fossil into items such as gems, ores and coins. You can also turn it into **Sturdy Fossil**, which can be used to forge cool weapons and armour. For more on using Desert Fossil, see page 27 of the *Crafting and Construction Handbook*.

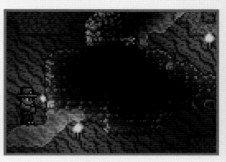

A stash of Desert Fossil

Dear diary: jackpot!

YOUR VERY OWN EXTRACTINATOR

Speaking of the **Extractinator**, you can usually find one lying around in the Underground Desert's abandoned cabins, or in **Golden Chests**. Make sure to pick one up to bring back to your base for efficient Desert Fossil processing.

A TOOTHY FRIEND

If you're really lucky when processing Desert Fossil, you might get an **Amber Mosquito**. And you know what you can do with the DNA in a mosquito trapped in Amber, right? Clone dinosaurs, of course! Equip it in your Pet slot to get your very own **baby dinosaur**.

CREEPY CRAWLERS

One of the things that makes the Underground Desert so dangerous is the creeps known as **Tomb Crawlers**. They'll spring out of the wall when you least expect it, and their heads pack quite a punch. You can tell they're getting nearer by the sounds of burrowing getting louder.

THE CORRUPTION

Welcome to evil biome number one, the Corruption . . . where everything is trying to kill you. And it will too, unless you already have some decent armour and weapons! Make sure to have at least **Gold** or **Platinum Armor** before you explore the depths of the Corruption.

MONSTER SPOTTERS' GUIDE

MONSTER	NOTES
Eater of Souls	Can drop Rotten Chunk and Ancient Armor
Devourer	Drops Worm Tooth and sometimes Rotten Chunk

NATURAL RESOURCES

 Ebonwood
 Vile Mushroom
 Deathweed
 Ebonstone Block
 Copper Ore
 Tin Ore
 Iron Ore

 Lead Ore
 Gems
 Life Crystal

FISHING GUIDE

 Bass
 Ebonkoi
 Balloon Pufferfish
 Bomb Fish
 Frog Leg
 Purple Clubberfish
 Zephyr Fish

 Corrupt Crate

UNIQUE SIGHTS

THAT'S NO RABBIT HOLE

As if the Eaters of Souls weren't enough, you need to look where you're going while in the Corruption; the place is filled with deep chasms, and there's no way you'll bounce when you reach the bottom. Come equipped with plenty of **rope** and a good **grappling hook**.

I HAVE A BAD FEELING ABOUT THIS

If you do survive a trip to the bottom of the Corruption's chasms, you'll encounter mysterious-looking **Shadow Orbs** encased in Ebonstone. You won't be able to mine Ebonstone Blocks at first, but you can buy **Purification Powder** from the **Dryad** and turn them into simple stone. **Bombs, Sticky Bombs** or **dynamite** will also do the trick.

Destroying a Shadow Orb with explosives or a hammer will get you some great weapons, but it will also trigger the possibility of a **meteorite** crashing on your world. Not only that, but if you have more than 200 Health you might get a visit from the **Goblin Army**.

Looks evil ... Better poke it with something sharp.

EVIL CRAFTING

The bottoms of chasms in the Corruption sometimes contain **Demon Altars**. These are special crafting stations that allow you to craft boss-summoning items, such as the **Suspicious Looking Eye** or the **Slime Crown**. They also become important once you reach Hardmode, as smashing them will generate Hardmode ores.

EARLY BIRD GETS THE GIANT WORM

Remember that chill running down your spine when you shattered a **Shadow Orb**? That'd be a giant evil worm flying at your face! Destroy three Shadow Orbs and the **Eater of Worlds** will pay you a visit. He's a tough boss to beat, but he'll reward you with precious **Shadow Scale** and **Demonite Ore**. Use these to craft superior armour, weapons and tools.

THE CRIMSON

If you thought the Corruption sounded bad, wait till you visit this flesh-themed nightmare. The two biomes are roughly equivalent, but with totally different rewards and ways to meet a messy death. Again, make sure you have **Silver** or **Tungsten Armor** before coming here.

MONSTER SPOTTERS' GUIDE

MONSTER	NOTES
Blood Crawler	
Face Monster	Sometimes drop Vertebrae
Crimera	

NATURAL RESOURCES

Shadewood	Vicious Mushroom	Deathweed	Crimstone Block
Copper Ore	Tin Ore	Iron Ore	Lead Ore

FISHING GUIDE

Bass	Crimson Tigerfish	Hemopiranha	Balloon Pufferfish
Bomb Fish	Frog Leg	Zephyr Fish	Crimson Crate

UNIQUE SIGHTS

ONE MESSED-UP CAVE

The Crimson features its own networks of caves that will lead to some nasty surprises underground. While they won't drop you straight to your death like the Corruption's chasms, it's still a good idea to bring **rope** and a **grappling hook** – especially if you intend to leave the way you came.

BE STILL, MY CRIMSON HEART
Deep in the Crimson's tunnels you'll find glowing **Crimson Hearts** encased in Crimstone. As with Ebonstone in the Corruption, you can use **Purification Powder** or explosives like **bombs**, **Sticky Bombs** or **dynamite** to clear the way. Hit a Crimson Heart with a hammer to destroy it and reap some good rewards.

Watch out though – as with Shadow Orbs, destroying a Crimson Heart might trigger a **meteorite crash** or the **Goblin Army** event!

FLESH AND BLOOD
The Crimson's evil crafting station, the **Crimson Altar**, can be found throughout the biome's tunnels. You can use it to craft boss-summoning items such as the **Bloody Spine**, which can then be used to call the Brain of Cthulhu. As with the Demon Altars, smashing Crimson Altars once you reach Hardmode will spread Hardmode ores.

BRAIN THE SIZE OF THE UNIVERSE
Smash three **Crimson Hearts** and the monstrosity known as the **Brain of Cthulhu** will show up to dissuade you from further damaging his property. It's a tough fight, but the **Crimtane Ore** and **Tissue Sample** you'll get as rewards are more than worth it.

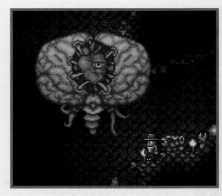

Something on your mind?

OCEAN

On both sides of your world is the deep shark-infested Ocean. You'll find some cool rewards waiting for you at the bottom ... if you manage not to drown!

MONSTER SPOTTERS' GUIDE

MONSTER	NOTES
Pink Jellyfish	Drops glowstick and sometimes Jellyfish Necklace
Crab	Found in water and on land
Sea Snail	Drops Purple Mucos
Squid	Drops black ink
Shark	Drops shark fin and sometimes diving helmet

NATURAL RESOURCES

Palm Wood

Coral

Seashell

Starfish

Copper Ore

Tin Ore

Iron Ore

Lead Ore

FISHING GUIDE

Pink Jellyfish

Red Snapper

Shrimp

Trout

Tuna

Balloon Pufferfish

Bomb Fish

Frog Leg

Reaver Shark

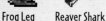
Sawtooth Shark

Swordfish

Zephyr Fish

Wooden Crate

Iron Crate

Gold Crate

UNIQUE SIGHTS

A NAPPING FRIEND

When you reach the Ocean for the first time, look out for my friend the **Angler** taking a nap near or on the Ocean surface. If you wake him up and have a house for him to move into, he'll make it his pleasure to annoy you with daily fishing quests. See the **Fishing** section on page 68 for details.

He's literally sleeping with the fishes.

UNDER THE SEA

You can reach the very bottom of the Ocean safely by using a **Gills Potion** or by getting a **Breathing Helmet** from sharks. Once there, you'll find **Water Chests** containing tons of useful items, including the **Breathing Reed**, which will let you hold your breath longer, and the **flipper**, an accessory that lets you swim back to the surface with ease.

MINING WITH THE FISHES

One of the best pickaxes available before Hardmode can be obtained using just a fishing pole and a little bit of patience. Make sure to boost your **fishing power** beforehand, as it helps you to catch the elusive **Reaver Shark** – a pickaxe so powerful you can even mine the first Hardmode ores with it!

JUNGLE

It might be pretty to look at, but everything in the Jungle wants to bite your face off. You'll want **Silver** or **Tungsten Armor** equipped before you head here – unless you want to feed the poor starving piranhas. Hey, they have to eat too.

MONSTER SPOTTERS' GUIDE

MONSTER	NOTES
Jungle Slime	Tougher than regular Slimes
Jungle Bat	Sometimes drops depth meter
Snatcher	Can attack through walls
Piranha	Sometimes drops hook, Robot Hat or compass

NATURAL RESOURCES

Rich Mahogany Moonglow Sky Blue Flower Copper Ore Tin Ore Iron Ore Lead Ore

FISHING GUIDE

Bass Double Cod Neon Tetra Balloon Pufferfish Bomb Fish Frog Leg Zephyr Fish

Jungle Crate

UNIQUE SIGHTS

DOCTOR BONES, I PRESUME

If you're lucky, one night you may encounter a zombie called **Doctor Bones**, who bears an uncanny resemblance to a famous archaeologist. If you put the poor undead fellow out of his misery, you'll get an Achievement called **Archaeologist**. If you're really lucky, you might even get his hat.

No, YOU belong in a museum!

GRUBBY, SLUGGY AND BUGGY

While slashing the Jungle's long grass, you'll eventually encounter three funny-looking grubs called **Sluggy**, **Grubby** and **Buggy**. You can combine the three in a cooking pot to craft **Grub Soup**. The dish might not sound too appealing, but it will grant you the Well Fed buff for a whopping thirty minutes. You can also use the three of them as fishing bait.

Buggy, running for its life

RECIPE	INGREDIENTS	CRAFTING STATION
Grub Soup (1)	Grubby (1) Sluggy (1) Buggy (1)	Cooking Pot

VOYAGE TO THE CENTRE OF THE EARTH

The Jungle biome features caves that extend deep, deep underground. So deep, in fact, that you can often reach the **Underground Jungle** without mining a single block. Make sure you have the best equipment available to you, as the monsters you'll find there are pretty tough! See the **Underground Jungle** section over the page for details.

A ROSE BY ANY OTHER NAME

While you're busy slashing grass and hunting for Grubby and its siblings, you might encounter red flowers that will drop the **Jungle Rose** when cut. This is a Vanity item that will show your default haircut with a rose in it.

I'm a pretty flower!

UNDERGROUND JUNGLE

Lush and vibrant, the Underground Jungle is one of the deadliest environments in Terraria. Make sure you have **Shadow** or **Crimson Armor** equipped before visiting, unless you're itching to fertilize the soil with some of your bones.

MONSTER SPOTTERS' GUIDE

MONSTER	NOTES
Spiked Jungle Slime	Shoots poisoned spikes, sometimes drops Stingers
Hornet	Can drop Stinger, Bezoar or Ancient Cobalt Armor
Man Eater	Can drop vine or Ancient Cobalt Armor
Jungle Bat	Sometimes drops depth meter
Piranha	Can drop hook, Robot Hat or compass
Lac Beetle	Drops Violet Husk (dye ingredient)

NATURAL RESOURCES

 Rich Mahogany
 Moonglow
 Sky Blue Flower
 Jungle Spores
 Iron Ore
 Lead Ore
 Silver Ore

 Tungsten Ore
 Gold Ore
 Platinum Ore
 Demonite Ore (rare)
 Crimtane Ore (rare)
 Obsidian
 Gems

 Life Crystal

FISHING GUIDE

 Armored Cavefish
 Bass
 Blue Jellyfish
 Golden Carp
 Honeyfin (from honey)
 Neon Tetra
 Stinkfish

 Variegated Lardfish
 Balloon Pufferfish
 Bomb Fish
 Frog Leg
 Rockfish
 Zephyr Fish
 Jungle Crate

UNIQUE SIGHTS

THE ROOTS RUN DEEP

The soil is so fertile in the Underground Jungle that trees even grow underground! They're difficult to spot in the darkness of the caves, but **Living Mahogany Trees** can be found throughout the Cavern layer. Seek their roots for an **Ivy Chest** containing such cool items as the **Staff of Regrowth**, which you can use to harvest herbs or grow grass. You may also find the **Anklet of the Wind**, which increases your movement speed, or the **Flower Boots**, which make flowers grow when you walk on grass.

An Ivy Chest in the roots of a Living Mahogany Tree

ANCIENT SHRINES

Another place to look for Ivy Chests is in **Jungle Shrines**. These rare structures can be easily identified by the **Green Torch** placed inside. Keep your eyes peeled!

A Green Torch marks the spot.

A MYSTERIOUS TEMPLE

Wander around the Underground Jungle long enough, and you'll run into a mysterious structure that you can't mine through with any of the pre-Hardmode pickaxes. This is the **Lihzahrd Temple**, and you won't be able to access it until you defeat the Hardmode boss known as **Plantera**. See the **Lihzahrd Temple** section on page 64 for details!

DON'T BREATHE THAT IN

Jungle Spores are a great ingredient used to craft powerful items such as the **Thorn Chakram**, the **Blade of Grass** or the **Amazon yo-yo**. Look for small glowing orbs throughout the Underground Jungle; you can collect these spores by hitting them with your pickaxe.

These smaller environments still offer plenty of business opportunities for the industrious mind.

LIVING TREE

Living Trees are gigantic tree-like structures that sometime grow on the surface. If you spot one it's well worth exploring its roots, as they sometimes contain valuable treasure.

UNIQUE SIGHTS

LIVING TREE CONSTRUCTION SET

Under some Living Trees you'll find one long, deep root that may lead to a small underground room. These rooms contain some Living Wood furniture as well as a **Living Wood Chest**. This chest will always contain a **Leaf Wand** and **Living Wood Wand**, and sometimes a **Living Loom** as well.

UNIQUE TREASURE

Leaf Wand

Living Wood Wand

Living Loom

You can use the wands to create your own Living Tree-like structures, as they convert **wood** into the materials that make up Living Trees: **Living Wood** and **Leaf Blocks**. As for the Living Loom, it will allow you to craft Living-Wood-themed furniture of your own.

I will call it Mini-Tree.

ENCHANTED SWORD SHRINE

These mini-biomes don't appear in every world, and even if they do, there's no guarantee you're going to get lucky with them. Still, given the amazing treasure that they give, definitely check them out as soon as you spot them.

UNIQUE TREASURE

Enchanted Sword

Arkhalis

Spotting a vertical shaft leading to an Enchanted Sword Shrine

UNIQUE SIGHTS

Enchanted Sword Shrines start a little below the surface as deep, narrow, vertical shafts. If you spot one of these, dig down until you find a sword in the stone below. Now it's time to cross your fingers!

Two times out of three you'll get a greyish-looking sword. Sorry! You lost and get nothing. But if you find a sword with a red-and-blue handle, then you, my friend, are about to make a profit.

Fake sword (left) and Enchanted Sword (right)

Nine times out of ten, you'll get a super-cool **Enchanted Sword**, a melee weapon that swings automatically when you hold the mouse button and fires a sword projectile. But if you're really lucky, you'll get the powerful **Arkhalis**: an extremely rare weapon that deals super-fast damage to nearby enemies!

Swinging the Arkhalis

UNDERGROUND MUSHROOM

You'll find these underground Mushroom Caves anywhere below the surface. They're worth seeking out for their **Glowing Mushrooms**, which you can use in a number of crafting recipes.

MONSTER SPOTTERS' GUIDE

MONSTER	NOTES
Fungi Bulb	Can attack through walls
Anomura Fungus	Resistant to knockback
Mushi Ladybugs	High health and damage

NATURAL RESOURCES

Glowing Mushroom

UNIQUE SIGHTS

MUSHROOM MADNESS

You can make everything from a **Mushroom Clock** to a **Mushroom Bathtub** using Glowing Mushrooms, but two of the most useful recipes are for **Healing Potions** and **Mana Potions**. Glowing Mushrooms grow back in no time, so don't worry about running out! Take as many as you can carry!

RECIPE	INGREDIENTS	CRAFTING STATION
Healing Potion (1)	Lesser Healing Potion (2) Glowing Mushroom (1)	Placed Bottle
Mana Potion (1)	Lesser Mana Potion (2) Glowing Mushroom (1)	

MUSHROOM BIOME STARTER KIT

Not only is the Underground Mushroom biome a great source of **Glowing Mushrooms**, you can even pick up a supply of **Mushroom Grass Seeds** to start your own mushroom-growing business! If you place Mushroom Grass Seeds on a stretch of a hundred tiles of Mud Blocks, this will eventually turn into a **Surface Mushroom biome!**

SPIDER NEST

These creepy nests are filled with hairy spiders that would like nothing better than to eat you for breakfast. Ask the Skeleton Merchant about it some time . . . He wasn't always a skeleton, you know. Shudder.

MONSTER SPOTTERS' GUIDE

MONSTER	NOTES
Wall Creeper	Can cross gaps by crawling on background wall

NATURAL RESOURCES

Cobweb

UNIQUE SIGHTS

BOUND IN STYLE

Somewhere in the Spider Nest is the **Stylist**, our friendly ally who went exploring spider nests all on her own. Free her from the webs and she'll move into a free house and let you change your hairstyle for a fee. Hey, we all need to make a living!

Do you happen to have a pair of scissors on you?

GRANITE CAVE

These dark caves, found in the Underground and Cavern layers, contain all the **Granite Blocks** you could ever hope for . . . as well as two unique enemies. They're more dangerous than the rest of the Underground, so proceed with caution.

MONSTER SPOTTERS' GUIDE

MONSTER	NOTES
Granite Golem	Drop Granite Block, can drop
Granite Elemental	Night Vision Helmet

NATURAL RESOURCES

Granite Block

UNIQUE SIGHTS

SEEING IN THE DARK

Once in a while, if you're lucky, a Granite Golem or Granite Elemental will drop a **Night Vision Helmet**. This helmet doesn't generate its own light like the mining helmet; it amplifies existing lights, just like the **Night Owl Potion**.

Light from a single torch without the Night Vision Helmet

Light with the Night Vision Helmet

MARBLE CAVE

Marble may look posh and classy, but Marble Caves contain some of the deadliest monsters in the game! Make sure you're ready for a challenge when you step inside, as the **Hoplites** can make short work of even the strongest adventurer.

MONSTER SPOTTERS' GUIDE

MONSTER	NOTES
Hoplite	Can drop Gladiator Armor or javelin

NATURAL RESOURCES

Marble Block

UNIQUE SIGHTS

THIS IS SPARTA!
Skeletons from another time period are always bad news – I'm looking at you, Undead Vikings – but the **Hoplites** and their javelins are especially nasty. Kill enough of them, though, and you'll be able to collect **Gladiator Armor** and look regal on the battlefield.

BEE HIVE

Spread throughout the **Underground Jungle** are Bee Hives, where you can stock up on life-restoring **honey** and even face off against the powerful **Queen Bee** herself.

MONSTER SPOTTERS' GUIDE

MONSTER	NOTES
Bee	Appears when hitting hive blocks; inflicts Poisoned debuff

NATURAL RESOURCES

Hive   Honey

FISHING GUIDE

You can catch **Honeyfins** by casting your line in honey. These guys are really worth the effort if you want to boost your Health (which you do!). See page 72 for more info from the Angler.

UNIQUE SIGHTS

MUMMY IS VERY CROSS

In each Bee Hive is a **larva** – and if you can't spot it, it's probably submerged in honey somewhere. If you hit it with a weapon or a pickaxe, you'll smash the larva, summoning an angry and buzzing **Queen Bee**.

She's a tough fight, but if you manage to defeat Queen Bee, you'll gain some unique, bee-themed items like the **Bee Gun**, the **Bee's Knees** and the **Hive Wand**.

One useful tip when fighting Queen Bee is to stand in **honey**, which will increase your health regeneration. And make sure to catch a few **Honeyfins** beforehand for a healing boost!

Can't find the Queen Bee? Craft yourself an **Abeemination**, and use it in the Jungle or Underground Jungle to summon her!

RECIPE	INGREDIENTS	CRAFTING STATION
Abeemination (1)	Honey Block (5) Stinger (1) Hive (5) Bottled Honey (1)	By Hand

METEORITE

Once you destroy your first **Crimson Heart** or **Shadow Orb**, you'll be presented with another opportunity for adventure: a **meteorite crash site**. You'll know it's time to go look for the crash site when the message 'A meteorite has landed!' appears on your screen.

MONSTER SPOTTERS' GUIDE

MONSTER	NOTES
Meteor Head	Can move through walls

NATURAL RESOURCES

Meteorite

UNIQUE SIGHTS

IT BURNS!
Meteorite is a cool and useful resource, but mining it isn't without its difficulties. When placed, the ore will burn to the touch; make sure to have either an **Obsidian Skin Potion**, **Obsidian Skull** or **Obsidian Shield** to resist the burning effect, or mine meteorite carefully without touching it.

For more tips on how to mine meteorite, see the section on meteorite on page 32 of the *Crafting and Construction Handbook*.

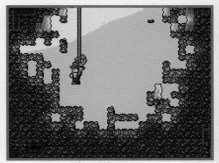

Careful now . . .

About to experience a burning sensation

FLAME ON
Another hazard of mining meteorite is the slow-moving but persistent **Meteor Heads** that swarm the place. They pack quite a punch, and will gladly knock you into the meteorite for a fiery death. Make sure to dispatch them before they get too close!

CHAPTER FOUR:
THE DUNGEON

Get rich or die trying! Or maybe a little bit of both.

UNLOCKING THE DUNGEON

The Dungeon is a massive underground structure located at one end of your map. If you can make your way inside, you'll battle hordes of undead creatures in a thrilling dungeon adventure! You might die a lot too. That tends to happen in the Dungeon.

PREPARATIONS

The Dungeon is one of the toughest biomes in pre-Hardmode Terraria, so you need to come prepared. You should have at least a **Shadow** or **Crimson Armor** set, plus a really good weapon. The Old Man will advise you not to fight **Skeletron** unless you have 300 Health and 10 Defense.

Ranged weapons such as bows work best against Skeletron. Try to get the **Demon** or **Tendon Bow**, and stock up on **Unholy Arrows**. Finally, make sure to have plenty of **Healing Potions** on hand and prepare for a tough fight.

DEFEATING SKELETRON

Once you're ready to face the Old Man's curse, head for the Dungeon at night. Talk to the Old Man, and Skeletron will appear. Here we go!

Skeletron just wants to hug you . . . to death!

Your first concern when fighting Skeletron is the hands. They are harder to dodge than the head, but the damage they deal adds up over time. Take them out quickly, making sure to avoid Skeletron's attacks. Soon you'll have only the head to deal with.

Skeletron's head going for a spin

Once you're down to the head, take your time! Skeletron's head is slower, but the damage it deals is deadly. Avoid it carefully and take down its Health; again, ranged weapons work best here. You can do it!

Rest in pieces!

TIPS

Don't get discouraged if you can't beat Skeletron on your first try! He's the hardest boss before Hardmode, so of course he's going to be a challenge. If you're having difficulty beating him, upgrade your equipment as much as you can, or try to experiment with different attack styles to find the one that works the best for you. For instance, if you keep running out of time, make sure to talk to the Old Man as the sun sets, so you can spend the entire night fighting.

If you have trouble moving around and dodging in the entrance, give yourself more space by building a wide arena out of platforms on top of the Dungeon. Remember to put down **campfires** and **Heart Lanterns** to help regenerate your health.

Don't worry if you fail: Skeletron is quite the challenge. Just try again and learn to dodge his attacks better. You'll have him beaten in no time!

EXPLORING THE DUNGEON

Congratulations, you beat Skeletron! Your challenges are far from over, though. The Dungeon is teeming with bloodthirsty monsters and deadly traps. And treasure! Did I mention treasure?

MONSTER SPOTTERS' GUIDE

MONSTER	NOTES
Angry Bones	Can open doors
Dark Caster	Can fire through walls and teleport
Cursed Skull	Can fly through walls
Dungeon Slime	Always drops a Golden Key

NATURAL RESOURCES

Ancient Necro Helmet   Alchemy Table   Aqua Scepter   Bewitching Table   Blue Moon   Bone   Bone Wand

Bone Welder   Clothier Voodoo Doll   Cobalt Shield   Handgun   Magic Missile   Muramasa   Nazar

 Tally Counter   Valor

CRAFTING TIP

Did you craft yourself an **Obsidian Skull** already? Save yourself some space and combine it with the Cobalt Shield to create the **Obsidian Shield**!

FISHING GUIDE

Water is rare in the Dungeon, so you'll probably need to create an artificial pond by bringing **water buckets** or using a **Bottomless Water Bucket**. The types of fish you can catch depends on your depth (Surface, Underground or Cavern layers), but you can always catch a **Dungeon Crate**, which may contain a **Golden Lock Box**.

UNIQUE SIGHTS

SPLISH SPLASH

One very useful weapon you can get from the Dungeon is the **Water Bolt**. You'll find it on shelves throughout the Dungeon: look for a blue book with a yellow band. Not only does the Water Bolt bounce off walls, it can hit multiple enemies too, making it especially useful against the Dungeon's skeleton hordes.

A Water Bolt on a dungeon shelf

STRIKING GOLD

Golden Chests contain some of the rarest and most unique treasure in Terraria, but you'll need a **Golden Key** to open them. These you can get from any monster in the Dungeon, but the **Dungeon Slime** drops one every time. Inside the chests you'll find powerful items like the **Muramasa**, an ingredient of the legendary sword, **Night's Edge**, and the **Cobalt Shield**, an essential component of the **Ankh Shield**.

A LOST FRIEND

Somewhere in the Dungeon, an ally is waiting for you to rescue her. You can free the **Mechanic** with a quick conversation, and – if you have an available house – she'll move right in. Just don't go spending all your money on wires! You'll need some gold for my wares too.

CLASSY FURNITURE

You wouldn't know by looking at them, but skeletons are great interior decorators. You'll find all sorts of interesting pieces of furniture around the Dungeon, including **pianos** and **bookcases**. And keep an eye out for the **Bewitching Table** and the **Alchemy Table**. The Bewitching Table lets you summon one extra minion for ten minutes, while the Alchemy Table works just like a Placed Bottle, except sometimes it won't consume your ingredients. Both will be nice additions to your base!

CHAPTER FIVE:
THE SPACE LAYER

Space! Exciting until you realize that everything that goes up must come down.

FLOATING ISLANDS

The Space layer is the uppermost point in Terraria, but there's not much to do up here except bounce around in reduced gravity. Just below Space, sandwiched between this layer and the Surface layer, are a few **Floating Islands** filled with unique treasures like the **Shiny Red Balloon**, the **Starfury**, the **Lucky Horseshoe** or the **Sky Mill**.

MONSTER SPOTTERS' GUIDE

MONSTER	NOTES
Harpy	Can drop feather or Giant Harpy Feather

NATURAL RESOURCES

Daybloom   Yellow Marigold   Silver Ore

Tungsten Ore   Gold Ore   Platinum Ore

FISHING GUIDE

Bass   Damselfish   Golden Carp

Balloon Pufferfish   Bomb Fish   Frog Leg

Zephyr Fish

REACHING FLOATING ISLANDS

GRAVITATION POTION

An easy way to reach Floating Islands is by using a **Gravitation Potion**. Look for **feathers** in **pots** and **chests** underground; you can use these to craft your first few potions, then gather some more from the **harpies** you'll run into on the Floating Islands.

There goes gravity!

To use the Gravitation Potion, activate it and press 'Up' to reverse gravity. The world will flip upside down and you will 'fall' into the sky. You can reverse gravity again when you're up in space, and then 'fall' left or right to move around and explore until you find a Floating Island. Make sure to kill plenty of harpies while you're up there so you can stock up on potion ingredients!

RECIPE	INGREDIENTS	CRAFTING STATION
Gravitation Potion (1)	Bottled Water (1) Fireblossom (1) Deathweed (1) Blinkroot (1) Feather (1)	Placed Bottle

SURVIVAL TIP

You might be falling into the sky, but you'll still die if you hit something solid at the end! If you don't have something like the **Lucky Horseshoe** to prevent damage on impact, make sure to reverse gravity a moment before you hit something, then reverse it again for a gentle fall.

TOWER AND SKY BRIDGE

If you're not having any luck crafting **Gravitation Potions**, or just like to build things, another method of discovering Floating Islands is a Sky Bridge. Build a tower out of simple material up into the sky. Then, when you're high enough, start building a bridge either left or right until you hit an island. Pay attention to your map, as some Floating Islands might appear higher or lower than your bridge.

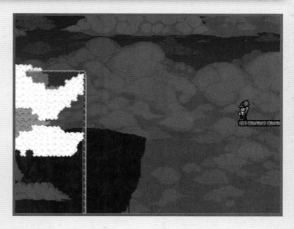

CHAPTER SIX:
THE UNDERWORLD LAYER

Welcome to Hell! You're not dead yet . . . but you will be if you don't watch your step.

THE UNDERWORLD

Dig down deep enough and you'll eventually hit the Underworld layer, a world of lava and nasty demon creatures. It's also the only source of precious **Hellstone**, so it's definitely worth risking a limb or two to retrieve it.

MONSTER SPOTTERS' GUIDE

MONSTER	NOTES
Lava Slime	Floats on lava
Hellbat	Can drop Magma Stone
Fire Imp	Sometimes drops Plumber's Hat or Obsidian Rose
Demon	Can drop Demon Scythe
Voodoo Demon	Drops Guide Voodoo Doll, can drop Demon Scythe
Bone Serpent	Can attack through walls

NATURAL RESOURCES

Fireblossom

Obsidian

Hellstone

FISHING GUIDE

It's impossible to fish in the Underworld before Hardmode. To learn how to do it once you're in Hardmode, see **Fishing in Lava** on page 72.

UNIQUE SIGHTS

FORGED IN HELL

The **ruined houses** you'll see throughout the Underworld contain a variety of unique furniture and items including the **Hellforge**. This crafting station can replace your furnace and can smelt Hellstone into Hellstone Bars. To pick it up, hit it with any **Pickaxe**, or simply hit the blocks underneath to make it fall.

HOT COMMODITY

The main reason to journey down to the Underworld is to mine **Hellstone**, but this is easier said than done. Not only does it burn to the touch, but every block you mine will leak a little bit of lava. To learn how to mine Hellstone safely, see the **Hellstone** section on page 34 of the *Crafting and Construction Handbook*.

Easy now . . .

THE SHADOW KNOWS

See those chests in the ruined houses of the Underworld? These **Shadow Chests** can only be unlocked with a **Shadow Key**, which you can find in the Dungeon's **Gold Chests**. They contain rare and unique treasure such as the **Dark Lance**, the **Flamelash**, the **Flower of Fire**, **Sunfury**, and the **Hellwing Bow**, as well as coins and items. They can even contain potions that can normally be found only in Hardmode, such as the **Lifeforce Potion** and the **Heartreach Potion**!

VOODOO CHILD

Notice something familiar with the small doll being dangled upside down by those flying **Voodoo Demons**? Why, it's our merry friend the Guide! Kill one of those demons to get the **Guide Voodoo Doll**, then drop it in lava to summon the final pre-Hardmode boss: the **Wall of Flesh**. Good luck!

Hey! Careful with that!

CHAPTER SEVEN:
HARDMODE BIOMES

When the going gets tough, the tough get richer.

WHAT IS HARDMODE?

Hardmode is a whole new difficulty level that unlocks once you defeat the **Wall of Flesh**. Once you enter Hardmode, there's no going back! All-new monsters, treasures and biomes will appear everywhere.

Remember the terror you felt when facing zombies on you first night in Terraria? You're about to experience it all over again. Exciting, isn't it?

PREPARING FOR HARDMODE

Because of how tough the monsters are when you first enter Hardmode, you should make sure you've got everything you possibly can before you unlock it. Make sure your **weapons**, **armour** and **items** are the best you can find.

UNLOCKING HARDMODE

Ready for the big time? Head to the **Underworld**, acquire a **Guide Voodoo Doll** from a Voodoo Demon and toss it in lava. Yes, this *will* kill the poor Guide, and he's never done anything to you. But you can't make omelettes without breaking a few eggs, am I right? Now get ready for the fight of your life!

The Wall of Flesh has awakened!

EFFECTS OF HARDMODE

Immediately upon beating the Wall of Flesh, two diagonal bands of **Hallow** and either **Corruption** or **Crimson** will spread from the Underworld layer all the way to Space. This will create entirely new biomes along the way: the **Underground Hallow, Corruption** and **Crimson**, as well as a surface **Hallow** biome.

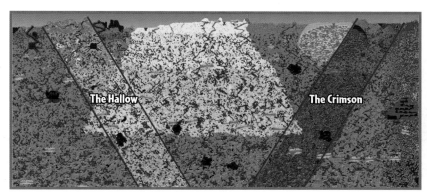

New Hallow and Crimson biomes created by unlocking Hardmode

HARDMODE ORES

Just as Hardmode offers new challenges, there are also many new opportunities for fun and profit in the form of items, treasures, and precious materials. See that **Pwnhammer** you got from the Wall of Flesh? Swing it at a **Shadow Altar** or **Crimson Altar** to shatter it and spread new ores throughout the world. There's literally no risk involved!*

* Some restrictions may apply. Shattering Evil Altars is likely to spread the Hallow, Corruption or Crimson further throughout your world. Also, evil wraiths will come out of nowhere and try to kill you. By using the Pwnhammer you absolve the Traveling Merchant of any and all civil or criminal liabilities resulting from said usage.

THE HALLOW

This is a new biome filled with **pixies** and **unicorns**! Sounds fantastic, right? Well ... unfortunately everything in the Hallow is out to kill you in the most unpleasant manner possible. You shouldn't stick around this biome for too long until you've had a chance to craft some armour and weapons with Hardmode ores.

MONSTER SPOTTERS' GUIDE

MONSTER	NOTES
Pixie	Drops Pixie Dust Can drop Fast Clock or megaphone
Unicorn	Drops Unicorn Horn Can drop Unicorn on a Stick
Rainbow Slime*	Drops gel and Rainbow Brick
Gastropod**	Drops gel

* During rain   ** At night only

NATURAL RESOURCES

Pearlwood   Mushroom   Copper Ore   Tin Ore   Iron Ore   Lead Ore

FISHING GUIDE

Bass   Princess Fish   Prismite   Balloon Pufferfish   Bomb Fish   Crystal Serpent   Frog Leg

Zephyr Fish   Hallowed Crate

UNIQUE SIGHTS

RAINBOWS AND UNICORNS

All monsters in the Hallow have a small chance of dropping a **Blessed Apple**. Equip it on your Special Equipment screen for an ultra-fast **Unicorn Mount**! After you defeat Plantera, if you manage to get a **Rainbow Gun** from a Hallowed Chest in the Hardmode Dungeon, you can fire it off while riding your unicorn for a special Achievement, **Rainbows and Unicorns**.

Rainbow power!

UNICORN ON A STICK

If you don't have the patience to get a Blessed Apple but still want to impress your friends, hunt unicorns until you get a **Unicorn on a Stick** . . . which you can use to have your own totally realistic Unicorn Mount! And if they believe that's the real thing, send them my way, will you? I have a bridge they might like to buy.

Giddy up!

UNDERGROUND HALLOW

If you thought the surface Hallow was a challenge, wait till you see the Underground Hallow: it's the kind of place where even the swords want to kill you. Avoid this area until you have upgraded your armour to at least **Mythril** or **Orichalcum Armor**.

MONSTER SPOTTERS' GUIDE

MONSTER	NOTES
Illuminant Slime	Can drop Blessed Apple
Illuminant Bat	
Chaos Elemental	Teleports; can drop Rod of Discord
Enchanted Sword	Attacks through blocks; can drop Nazar
Hallowed Mimic	Drops unique weapons and grappling hook

NATURAL RESOURCES

Crystal Shard   Copper Ore   Tin Ore   Iron Ore   Lead Ore   Silver Ore   Tungsten Ore

Gold Ore   Platinum Ore   Obsidian   Cobalt Ore   Palladium Ore   Mythril Ore   Orichalcum Ore

Adamantite Ore   Titanium Ore   Gems

NATURAL RESOURCES

Armored Cavefish   Bass   Chaos Fish   Flarefin Koi*   Golden Carp   Princess Fish   Prismite   Balloon Pufferfish

Bomb Fish   Crystal Serpent   Frog Leg   Obsidian Swordfish*   Rockfish   Scaly Truffle**   Zephyr Fish   Hallowed Crate

* Fished in lava using Hotline Fishing Rod   ** Only where Hallow, Cavern and Snow meet

UNIQUE SIGHTS

CRYSTAL CLEAR

One good reason to head down to the Underground Hallow is to collect **Crystal Shards**. These crystals glow in the dark, so you can easily spot them from a distance. You can use them in many recipes including **Greater Healing Potions** and **Super Mana Potions**, as well as for powerful weapons such as the **Phasesaber**, **Crystal Storm** and the **Chik** yo-yo.

Spotting a Crystal Shard from its glow

RECIPE	INGREDIENTS	CRAFTING STATION
Greater Healing Potion (1)	Pixie Dust (3), Bottled Water (3) Crystal Shard (1)	Placed Bottle
Super Mana Potion (15)	Greater Mana Potion (15), Fallen Star (1), Unicorn Horn (1), Crystal Shard (3)	
Phasesaber (1)	Phaseblade (1), Crystal Shard (50)	Mythril/Orichalcum Anvil
Chik (1)	Wooden Yo-yo (1), Crystal Shard (15), Soul of Light (10)	
Crystal Storm (1)	Spell Tome (1), Crystal Shard (20), Soul of Light (15)	Bookcase

WATCH YOUR FINGERS

The Underground Hallow is so nasty, even the chests here want to bite your arm off! Watch out if you spot a chest around these parts, as it might be a **Hallowed Mimic** in disguise. These monsters are tough to beat, but they drop powerful and unique items such as the **Daedalus Stormbow**, the **Flying Knife**, the **Crystal Vile Shard** or the **Illuminant Hook**.

WHEN PIGS FLY

If you find a spot in the Cavern layer where the Hallow and the Underground Snow biomes overlap, cast your line and cross your fingers: you might get lucky and catch a **Scaly Truffle**. By equipping this item in your Mount equipment slot, you can summon a **Pigron Mount**, an odd-looking creature that can fly for a limited time.

UNDERGROUND CORRUPTION

If you thought the Hallow biome was bad, wait until you see the upgraded evil biomes! The Underground Corruption has its own innovative ways of killing you, and plenty of enticing treasures to lure you there.

MONSTER SPOTTERS' GUIDE

MONSTER	NOTES
World Feeder	Attacks through walls, drops Cursed Flame
Cursed Hammer	Attacks through walls, can drop Nazar
Clinger	Shoots projectiles, drops Cursed Flame
Corruptor	Can drop vitamins
Corrupt Slime	Splits into three Slimelings at death
Slimer	Loses its wings when taking damage
Corrupt Mimic	Drops unique weapons and grappling hook

NATURAL RESOURCES

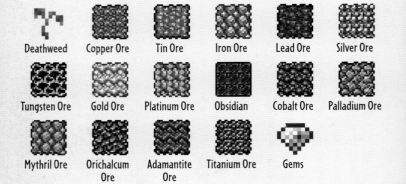

Deathweed   Copper Ore   Tin Ore   Iron Ore   Lead Ore   Silver Ore

Tungsten Ore   Gold Ore   Platinum Ore   Obsidian   Cobalt Ore   Palladium Ore

Mythril Ore   Orichalcum Ore   Adamantite Ore   Titanium Ore   Gems

FISHING GUIDE

 Armored Cavefish

 Bass

 Ebonkoi

 Flarefin Koi*

 Golden Carp

 Balloon Pufferfish

 Bomb Fish

 Frog Leg

Obsidian Swordfish*

Purple Clubberfish

Rockfish

Toxikarp

Zephyr Fish

 Corrupt Crate

* Fished in lava using Hotline Fishing Rod

UNIQUE SIGHTS

BITING THE HAND THAT LOOTS YOU

Just like the **Hallowed Mimics** in the Underground Hallow, **Corrupt Mimics** are mean monsters who disguise themselves as chests. Kill them to get some nice unique loot such as the **Dart Rifle**, the **Worm Hook**, the **Chain Guillotines** or the **Clinger Staff**, to name a few.

AGENTS OF SHIELD

The **Ankh Shield** is one of the most useful items in the game, and in the course of gathering all the ingredients needed to craft it, you'll spend a lot of time in the Underground Corruption. There are three ingredients to be found here: you can get the **blindfold** from Slimelings, the **Nazar** from Cursed Hammers and **vitamins** from Corruptors. Happy hunting!

CRAFTING TIP

To learn all about crafting the Ankh Shield, check out page 40 of the *Crafting and Construction Handbook*!

UNDERGROUND CRIMSON

Much like its counterpart the Corruption, Hardmode's **Crimson** now has all-new and fun ways to kill you in the blink of an eye. But you know what they say: no pain, no gain!

MONSTER SPOTTERS' GUIDE

MONSTER	NOTES
Crimson Axe	Can drop Nazar or meat grinder
Ichor Sticker	Drops Ichor
Floaty Gross	Attacks through walls, can drop vitamins or meat grinder
Crimson Mimic	Drops unique items and hook
Blood Feeder	Water enemy
Blood Jelly	

NATURAL RESOURCES

 Deathweed
 Copper Ore
 Tin Ore
 Iron Ore
 Lead Ore
 Silver Ore
 Tungsten Ore

 Gold Ore
 Platinum Ore
 Obsidian
 Cobalt Ore
 Palladium Ore
 Mythril Ore
Orichalcum Ore

 Adamantite Ore
 Titanium Ore
 Gems

NATURAL RESOURCES

 Armored Cavefish
 Bass
 Crimson Tigerfish
 Flarefin Koi*
 Golden Carp
 Hemopiranha
 Balloon Pufferfish

 Bladetongue
 Bomb Fish
 Frog Leg
 Obsidian Swordfish*
 Rockfish
 Zephyr Fish
 Crimson Crate

*Fished in lava using Hotline Fishing Rod

UNIQUE SIGHTS

A CHEST WITH TEETH
By now you know the drill: those chests in the Underground Crimson? Some of them want to eat you. Beat these tough monsters known as **Crimson Mimics** for a chance to get cool rewards such as **Life Drain**, the **Dart Pistol**, **Fetid Baghnakhs**, **Flesh Knuckles** or the **Tendon Hook**.

A chest with bad breath

AN AXE TO GRIND
Just like the Hallow and the Corruption, the Underground Crimson has its own nasty, spinning weapon that can charge at you through walls: the **Crimson Axe**. If you fancy having one of your own, the Crimson Axe looks just like the pre-Hardmode **Blood Lust Cluster**.

A Crimson Axe charging through solid blocks

RECIPE	INGREDIENTS	CRAFTING STATION
Blood Lust Cluster (1)	Crimtane Ore (10)	Iron/Lead Anvil

Sigh . . . Why does no one ever visit?

MACABRE FURNITURE
The creatures in the Underground Crimson can sometimes drop a unique crafting station with no equivalent for the Corruption. Hunt down the Floaty Grosses and Crimson Axes for a **meat grinder**, which you can use to turn Crimtane Blocks into **Flesh Blocks**. Using a **Flesh Cloning Vat**, you can then craft these into a variety of bloody furniture pieces that will surely delight your visitors.

HARDMODE DESERT

With the Hallow and either the Corruption or the Crimson spreading throughout your world, it's likely that your Desert biomes will be affected pretty quickly! Fortunately, with every crisis comes a business opportunity.

MONSTER SPOTTERS' GUIDE

MONSTER	NOTES
SURFACE	
Mummy	Can drop Fast Clock
Light Mummy	Hallow only Can drop Light Shard or Trifold Map
Dark Mummy	Corruption and Crimson only Can drop Dark Shard, megaphone or blindfold
UNDERGROUND	
Basilisk	Sometimes drops Sturdy Fossil
Sand Poacher	Drops 6 Silver Coins
Lamia	Can drop Sun Mask (normal version) or Moon Mask (Corruption/Crimson)
Dune Splicer	Can attack through walls
Desert Spirit	Throws homing projectiles
Ghoul	Corruption/Crimson variant can drop Dark Shard, Hallowed can drop Light Shard

NATURAL RESOURCES

Cactus   Desert Fossil   Waterleaf   Pink Prickly Pear   Iron Ore   Lead Ore   Silver Ore

Tungsten Ore   Gold Ore   Platinum Ore   Demonite Ore (rare)   Crimtane Ore (rare)   Cobalt Ore   Palladium Ore

Mythril Ore   Orichalcum Ore   Adamantite Ore   Titanium Ore   Gems   Life Crystal

FISHING GUIDE

As with the pre-Hardmode Desert, there isn't any special reason to fish in the Hardmode Desert . . . but if you *really* want to, just dig a hole and fill it with water.

 Armored Cavefish

 Bass

 Blue Jellyfish

 Golden Carp

 Green Jellyfish

 Balloon Pufferfish

 Bomb Fish

 Frog Leg

 Rockfish

 Zephyr Fish

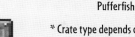 Crate*

* Crate type depends on whether fishing spot is uncorrupted or taken over by Corruption/Crimson/Hallow

UNIQUE SIGHTS

ARE YOU MY MUMMY?

In Hardmode your Desert is teeming with **mummies**, whether they're corrupted or not. These bandaged monstrosities are valuable sources of **Light Shards** and **Dark Shards**, but they also drop a cool Vanity set: the Mummy Costume. Collect the **Mummy Mask**, **Shirt** and **Pants** to be fully kitted out.

Why hello there, fellow mummy!

POW, RIGHT IN THE KISSER!

Speaking of **Light** and **Dark Shards**, they are the ingredients in a powerful and unique flail, the **Dao of Pow**. You'll also need a **Soul of Light** and a **Soul of Night** from the Underground Hallow and Underground Corruption/Crimson.

Yin-yang to the face!

RECIPE	INGREDIENTS	CRAFTING STATION
Dao of Pow (1)	Dark Shard (1) Light Shard (1) Soul of Light (7) Soul of Night (7)	Mythril/Orichalcum Anvil

HARDMODE JUNGLE

The Hardmode Jungle, especially the Underground Jungle, is undeniably the toughest biome in Terraria. Remember when you died repeatedly exploring the Underworld? If you dig deep enough in the Jungle, you'll be *relieved* to finally make it to Hell.

MONSTER SPOTTERS' GUIDE

MONSTER	NOTES
Angry Trapper	Can drop Uzi
Arapaima	Swimming enemy
Giant Tortoise	Can drop Turtle Shell
Angler Fish	Sometimes drops adhesive bandage or Robot Hat
SURFACE ONLY	
Derpling	Day only
Giant Flying Fox	Night only
UNDERGROUND ONLY	
Jungle Creeper	Can climb on background walls
Moth	Can drop Butterfly Dust
Moss Hornet	Sometimes drops Bezoar or Tattered Bee Wing

NATURAL RESOURCES

Rich Mahogany   Moonglow   Sky Blue Flower   Jungle Spores   Iron Ore   Lead Ore   Silver Ore

Tungsten Ore   Gold Ore   Platinum Ore   Demonite Ore (rare)   Crimtane Ore (rare)   Cobalt Ore   Palladium Ore

Mythril Ore   Orichalcum Ore   Adamantite Ore   Titanium Ore   Gems   Life Crystal   Life Fruit

FISHING GUIDE

Armored Cavefish

Bass

Blue Jellyfish

Flarefin Koi*

Golden Carp

Green Jellyfish

Honeyfin (from honey)

Neon Tetra

Obsidifish*

Stinkfish

Variegated Lardfish

Frog Leg

Balloon Pufferfish

Bomb Fish

Obsidian Swordfish*

Rockfish

Zephyr Fish

Jungle Crate

* From lava using Hotline Fishing Rod

UNIQUE SIGHTS

THE JUNGLE GROWS RESTLESS . . .

Once you summon and defeat the three Hardmode monstrosities known as the **Mechanical Bosses – the Destroyer**, **the Twins** and **Skeletron Prime** – strange bulbs will start to appear in the Underground Jungle. This is **Plantera's Bulb**: destroy it at your own peril, as Plantera itself will come calling!

GREEN ECONOMY

A second benefit of beating the Mechanical Bosses is the spread of **Chlorophyte** throughout the Underground Jungle. This precious ore grows on mud and will spread around the Jungle, ready to be forged into powerful armour and weaponry. You'll need the **Pickaxe Axe**, the drill known as **Drax**, or something better to mine it, though!

THE FRUITS OF LIFE

As you explore the Underground Jungle in Hardmode, you'll run into odd, heart-shaped plants. These are **Life Fruits**, and they grow even more frequent once you defeat one of the Mechanical Bosses. If you already have 400 Health from using **Life Crystals**, Life Fruits will raise your maximum Health by another five points, up to a maximum of 500.

LIHZAHRD TEMPLE

Wondering what lies beyond that mysterious temple gate deep in the Underground Jungle? Now's the time to find out! Once you defeat **Plantera** you'll get a **Temple Key** that will unlock this ancient place. Tread carefully!

MONSTER SPOTTERS' GUIDE

MONSTER	NOTES
Lihzahrd	Can drop Lihzahrd Power Cell, lizard egg or Solar Tablet
Flying Snake	Fragment

UNIQUE SIGHTS

IT'S A TRAP!
Lihzahrd people sure know their wiring! The place is teeming with deadly traps ranging from **Super Dart Traps** to **Flame Traps** and more. Don't believe me? Equip a **wrench** to make the wires visible and see for yourself. Make sure to disarm everything with a **wire cutter**, then bring some traps home to install in your own base!

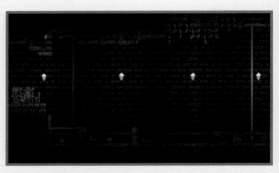

Three different traps visible with an equipped wrench

Facing Mothron and its progeny during a solar eclipse

TOTAL ECLIPSE
Throughout your Lihzahrd adventures you'll stumble upon **Solar Tablet Fragments**, which can be combined into a **Solar Tablet**. Although solar eclipses can occur on their own, using a Solar Tablet during daytime will trigger one right away. You'll get some great items from the monsters that will show up, including some of the most powerful in the game, but prepare for a long, dangerous day!

I'VE GOT THE POWER

Another mysterious object you'll encounter in the temple is the **Lihzahrd Power Cell**. This is used to summon the Hardmode boss known as **Golem** in the main chamber of the Lihzahrd Temple: just locate the glowing **Lihzahrd Altar** and use the Power Cell on it. Get ready for a tough fight!

ANCIENT TREASURE

A good place to look for **Lihzahrd Power Cells** and **Solar Tablets** is in the few **chests** you'll find scattered around the temple complex. Each **Lihzahrd Chest** contains a Lihzahrd Power Cell and may contain a **Lihzahrd Furnace**, a crafting station you can use to craft temple-themed furniture.

I AM THE LIZARD KING

You wouldn't think of the Lihzahrd Temple as a place to make friends, yet every time you kill a Lihzahrd or flying snake, there's a chance you'll get a **lizard egg**. Better be patient, though: the chances of getting an egg are only 1,000 to one!

HARDMODE DUNGEON

If you like your combat crazy and deadly, the Hardmode Dungeon is the place for you! The Dungeon will switch to all-new enemies as soon as you defeat **Plantera** for the first time. Come equipped with your best gear and plenty of potions; the Hardmode Dungeon won't give you a moment's rest.

MONSTER SPOTTERS' GUIDE

MONSTER	NOTES
Blue Armored Bones	Can drop Armor Polish
Rusty Armored Bones	Can drop adhesive bandage
Hell Armored Bones	Inflicts 'On Fire!' debuff
Paladin	Rare; can drop Paladin's Shield or Paladin's Hammer
Necromancer	
Ragged Caster	Can attack through walls
Diabolist	
Skeleton Commando	Sometimes drops rocket launcher
Skeleton Sniper	Can drop rifle scope or sniper rifle
Tactical Skeleton	Can drop SWAT Helmet or Tactical Shotgun
Giant Cursed Skull	Can move through walls
Bone Lee	Rare; sometimes drops black belt or Tabi
Dungeon Spirit	Always drops Ectoplasm

UNIQUE TREASURE

Adhesive Bandage · Armor Polish · Black Belt · Bone Feather · Ectoplasm · Inferno Fork · Keybrand

Kraken · Magnet Sphere · Paladin's Hammer · Paladin's Shield · Rifle Scope · Rocket Launcher · Shadowbeam Staff

Sniper Rifle · Spectre Staff · SWAT Helmet · Tabi · Tactical Shotgun · Wisp in a Bottle

UNIQUE SIGHTS

BIOME CHESTS

The Hardmode Dungeon contains some unique chests called **Biome Chests** that correspond to four major biomes of your world (Jungle, Snow, Hallow, and either Corruption or Crimson). To find the keys to each chest, you'll need to hunt monsters in their corresponding biome. Not all Biome Chests can be found in a given Dungeon, though. If you can't find the Biome Chest you're looking for on your own world, create new worlds and go check out their Dungeons. Skeletron should be no match for your awesome Hardmode weapons this time around!

Corruption Chest

BIOME CHEST		CONTENTS
	Jungle Chest	Piranha Gun
	Corruption Chest*	Scourge of the Corruptor
	Crimson Chest**	Vampire Knives
	Hallowed Chest	Rainbow Gun
	Frozen Chest	Staff of the Frost Hydra

* Appears only on Corruption worlds
** Appears only on Crimson worlds

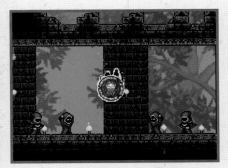

Guys, do you mind? Some of us have to go to work in the morning!

CULT OF THE MOON LORD

Once you defeat **Golem** back in the **Lihzahrd Temple**, a strange group of fanatics will start calling the Dungeon entrance their home. They're pushovers in a fight, but their boss, the **Lunatic Cultist**, is anything but. Beating the Lunatic Cultist and his followers is the start of the **Lunar Events**; if you manage to destroy the four **Celestial Towers** that appear around the world, the **Moon Lord,** Terraria's ultimate boss, will show up. Get ready for the fight of your life!

HARDMODE TIP

The Moon Lord is one tough boss to beat, my young friend. Check out the upcoming *Terraria: Hardmode Survival Handbook* if you need some help!

CHAPTER EIGHT:
THE ERRAND MONKEY'S GUIDE TO FISHING

By the Angler – World-Renowned Fish Expert and Master Fisherman

I bribed the Angler with a rare Jewelfish to get him to write this guide. I'm sure you'll find it useful if you can get past the Angler's attitude! He's a good kid, you know . . . He doesn't like to admit it, but I think he likes you – TM

Hey, you! Yeah, you'll do. Grab a fishing pole and off you go.

What's that, you want to learn how to fish? It's true that my last errand monkey got eaten by a Reaver Shark . . . Fine. To avoid wasting any more of my precious time, I'll share my hard-earned wisdom and experience about the wonderful world of fish and fishing. Get ready to be amazed!

You'd better listen carefully and take notes, because I'm not going to repeat myself! (Although I suppose you could just reread this guide.)

FISHING FOR BEGINNERS

To fish, you're going to need three things: water, a fishing pole and some bait. Think you'll remember that?

STEP ONE:
FIND SOME WATER

That part shouldn't be too hard. Make sure there are at least seventy-five tiles of water in the pool. Fish don't like hanging out in puddles, so there's no point casting your line there.

Absolute minimum size for fishing

STEP TWO: CAST YOUR LINE

Select your fishing pole and click anywhere on the water to cast your line. Sorry, am I going too quickly?

STEP THREE: WAIT FOR A BITE

See that fishing float? I know you want to click it. But don't. Just don't. Wait for it . . . Waaaaait for it . . .

STEP FOUR: REEL IT IN

When you see that fishing float bob, it means you've got a bite! (Don't get too excited . . . Given your skill level it's probably an old shoe.) Click to reel it in.

STEP FIVE: CELEBRATE!

You did it! You caught your first fish and it totally wasn't an old busted shoe! (Wait, was it? I wasn't paying attention.) Isn't that exciting? Whew! I need to lie down for a quick nap. Be right back.

Nailed it!

THE SCIENCE OF FISHING

So you thought that was simple? I was just dumbing it down for you!
There are actually tons of different factors that affect your fishing skill.

FISHING POLE
Determines your base fishing skill. Fishing power ranges from five per cent (Wood Fishing Pole) to fifty per cent (Golden Fishing Rod).

BAIT
Contributes to fishing skill. Bait power ranges from five per cent (Monarch Butterfly) to fifty per cent (Master Bait).

TIME OF DAY
Try fishing around sunrise or sunset. Noon and midnight tend to be less lucky.

WEATHER
Fish like rain, but they'll settle for cloudy weather. Sunny days are the worst.

MOON PHASE
You'll get better catches around the full moon – and will get a penalty on the new moon.

WATER SIZE
The bigger the water-pool size the better! You'll get a penalty to your fishing skill for any lake below 300 tiles in size.

FISHING ITEMS
Fetch me the fish I want and I might reward you with some choice items that boost your fishing power.

TO SUM UP
Always try and fish from a large lake with a Golden Fishing Rod and Master Bait at sunset on a rainy night with a full moon. Also, keep me happy. Piece of (fish)cake!

FISHING POLES

Huh? You don't know where to get a fishing pole? Can't you do anything by yourself? Here are four fishing poles you can craft on your own.

RECIPE	POWER	INGREDIENTS	CRAFTING STATION
Wood Fishing Pole (1)	5%	Wood (8)	Work Bench
Reinforced Fishing Pole (1)	15%	Lead/Iron Bar (8)	
Fisher of Souls (1)	20%	Demonite Bar (8)	Iron/Lead Anvil
Fleshcatcher (1)	22%	Crimtane Bar (8)	

FISHING POLE	POWER	NOTES
Fiberglass Fishing Pole	25%	In Underground Jungle
Mechanic's Rod*	30%	Sold by Mechanic
Sitting Duck's Fishing Pole	40%	Sold by Traveling Merchant
Hotline Fishing Hook*	45%	Fishing quest reward
Golden Fishing Pole	50%	

* Available in Hardmode only

BAIT

You can use pretty much every critter or bug for fishing. Just break rocks for worms or mow the grass with your sword, and catch whatever jumps out of the bushes with a **bug net**. Make sure to also look for **worms** during the rain, or **fireflies** at night.

You can buy a **bug net** from the Merchant and swing it at the critters you spot. Just like that!

A grasshopper making a run for it

Gotcha!

FISHING IN HONEY

The Nurse told me how you get banged up all the time, so I thought I'd share a fishing secret: head to the **Underground Jungle**, spot a **Bee Hive** and cast your line!

You see, honey is home to **Honeyfins**, a special kind of fish that gives back 120 Health when eaten. They're the second-best healing item before Hardmode, so they're definitely worth the trip to the Underground Jungle. Get to it!

Sweet!

FISHING IN LAVA

Terrarians! Tonight we fish . . . in Hell!

Noticed how there's no water down in the Underworld? That won't stop a serious fishing master! First, you'll need to jump through enough hoops for me that I decide you're worthy of the **Hotline Fishing Hook**. Don't even bother before **Hardmode**, by the way.

Once you've run enough errands for me, I'll give you the Hotline Fishing Hook. Now head to a lava spot and cast your line! You'll catch **Flarefin Koi** and **Obsidifish**, two ingredients of the **Inferno Potion** – which sets nearby enemies on fire!

Such a peaceful fishing spot . . .

RECIPE	INGREDIENTS	CRAFTING STATION
Inferno Potion (1)	Bottled Water (1) Flarefin Koi (1) Obsidifish (2) Fireblossom (1)	Placed Bottle

Inferno Potions: so hot right now

FISH YOU CAN USE

If you need a reason to fish besides how calming it is – and why would you? – consider this: it's also an endless source of useful items.

Here are some of the usable fish you can catch. Don't say I never did anything for you!

Cutting down trees with the Sawtooth Shark

ITEM	SOURCE	TYPE
Balloon Pufferfish		High-jump accessory
Bomb Fish	Any biome	Sticky Bomb
Frog Leg		Auto-jump accessory
Frost Daggerfish	Snow	Weapon
Honeyfin	Honey	Restores Health
Purple Clubberfish	Corruption	Weapon
Reaver Shark	Ocean	Pickaxe
Rockfish	Underground	Hammer
Sawtooth Shark	Ocean	Chainsaw
Swordfish	Ocean	Spear
Zephyr Fish	Any biome	Pet
HARDMODE ONLY		
Obsidian Swordfish	Lava	Spear
Scaly Truffle	(See 'Underground Hallow' for details)	Mount
Toxikarp	Corruption	
Bladetongue	Crimson	Weapon
Crystal Serpent	Hallow	

FISHING CRATES

Depending on the biome, you can sometimes catch a **crate** containing some useful loot. They all contain items as well as coins and ores.

ITEM	SOURCE	TYPE
Wooden Crate	Any	Common
Iron Crate		
Jungle Crate	Jungle	
Sky Crate	Sky	
Corrupt Crate	Corruption	Uncommon
Crimson Crate	Crimson	
Hallowed Crate*	Hallow	
Dungeon Crate	Dungeon	

FISHING QUESTS

Now let's discuss the best reason to fish: me!

I love fish of all sizes, colours and shapes! Come to me every day after **4:30 a.m.** and I'll give you a **fishing quest** worthy of your talent and intelligence. Just bring me back the fish I ask for before the next morning and I'll make it worth your while.

Word to the wise, though: I only give out one quest each day. Be a good little errand monkey and don't bother me once we're done for the day.

FISHING QUEST REWARDS

Helping me should be its own reward, of course. But in case you need a little convincing, here's the list of things you can get when you do what I say. I give most of these items at random, so make sure to come to me every day for a new quest!

In addition to all of these wonderful items, I also give out **coins** and either **Apprentice**, **Journeyman** or **Master Bait**. Exciting, isn't it? Now go get me that fish!

REWARD	DESCRIPTION	ODDS
Fuzzy Carrot	Summons Bunny Mount	on 5th quest
Angler Hat		on 10th quest
Angler Vest	Increases fishing level	on 15th quest
Angler Pants		on 20th quest
Golden Fishing Rod	50% fishing power	on 30th quest
Hotline Fishing Hook*	45% fishing power, can fish in lava	1/100 after 25th quest
Fin Wings*	Can fly	
Bottomless Water Bucket*	Infinite water bucket	1/70 after 10th quest
Super Absorbant Sponge*	Can absorb water	
Golden Bug Net	Improved bug net	1/80 chance
Fish Hook	Grappling hook	1/60 chance
High Test Fishing Line	Prevents line from breaking	
Angler Earring	+10% fishing power	
Tackle Box	Less chance of losing bait	
Mermaid Costume	Vanity items	1/40 chance
Fish Costume		
Fisherman's Pocket Guide	Shows fishing power	
Weather Radio	Shows weather	
Sextant	Shows phase of the moon	
Sonar Potion	Shows name of catch	
Fishing Potion	+15% fishing power	3/14 chance
Crate Potion	Increases odds of fishing crates	
Coralstone Block		
Bunnyfish Trophy		
Goldfish Trophy		
Sharkteeth Trophy		
Swordfish Trophy		
Treasure Map		
Seaweed Planter	Decorative items	1/88 chance
Pillagin Me Pixels		
Compass Rose		
Ship's Wheel		
Life Preserver		
Wall Anchor		
Ship in a Bottle		

* Hardmode only

THE ULTIMATE CATCH

So you think you're good at fishing? I've got news for you, pal ... You're nothing until you've caught the ultimate big fish: **Duke Fishron!**

SETTING THE BAIT

When in Hardmode, visit **Glowing Mushroom Caves** and look for Duke Fishron's favourite snack: **Truffle Worms**. Equip your **bug net** and charge at them: they bury into the ground as soon as they see you, so there's no time to waste!

A Truffle Worm

FACING THE DUKE

Once you're stocked up on Truffle Worms, grab your best equipment, head to the **Ocean**, and cast your line. Here comes the Duke!

Get ready for the battle of your errand-monkey life. Duke Fishron will throw **Detonating Bubbles** and **Sharknadoes** at you as he flies around and attacks at high speed. Dodge his attacks the best you can if you want to survive!

Man versus pig-dragon-fish! The ultimate battle!

REWARDS

Duke Fishron drops some of the best items in the whole game, including a powerful flail called **Flairon** that fires deadly bubbles, as well as the **Shrimpy Truffle**, an item you can only get in Expert mode that lets you summon a Cute Fishron Mount. Defeating the Duke is sure to give you an edge against the **Moon Lord** himself!

Flairon and Cute Fishron Mount

But most importantly, you'll earn my grudging respect. And isn't that worth more than anything?

TREASURE INDEX

Not sure of the purpose of an item mentioned in this guide? Look it up here!

PRE-HARDMODE TREASURE

ITEM	DESCRIPTION	SOURCE
Aglet	Increases movement speed	Forest
Alchemy Table	Crafting station	Dungeon
Amber Mosquito	Summons baby dinosaur pet	Extractinator
Ancient Cobalt Armor	17 Defense, reduces mana usage	Underground Jungle
Ancient Necro Helmet	5 Defense, counts towards Necro Armor set bonus	Dungeon
Anklet of the Wind	Increases movement speed	Underground Jungle
Antlion Mandible	Used to craft Sandgun and Mining Potion	Desert, Underground Desert
Aqua Sceptre	Magic weapon	Dungeon
Archaeologist's Hat	Vanity item	Jungle
Arkhalis	Very rare melee weapon	Enchanted Sword Shrines
Bewitching Table	Increases minion capacity when used	Dungeon
Bezoar	Grants immunity to poison	Underground Jungle
Black Ink	Dye ingredient	Ocean
Blizzard in a Bottle	Allows double-jump	Snow, Underground Snow
Blue Moon	Flail melee weapon	Dungeon
Bone	Ingredient in Necro Armor, pianos, bone furniture, etc.	Dungeon
Bone Wand	Places Bone Blocks in exchange for bones	Dungeon
Bone Welder	Crafting station for bone furniture	Dungeon
Breathing Reed	Increases breathing time underwater	Ocean
Chain Knife	Flail-like melee weapon	Cavern
Climbing Claws	Lets you slide down walls	Forest
Clothier Voodoo Doll	Summons Skeletron at night	Dungeon
Cloud in a Bottle	Allows double-jump	Underground, Cavern
Cobalt Shield	Protects from knockbacks	Dungeon
Compass	Displays horizontal position	Jungle, Underground, Underground Snow, Cavern
Marshmallow	Used to craft Marshmallow on a Stick	Snow
Crimtane Ore[1]	Used to craft Crimtane Bar	Underground (rare), Eye of Cthulhu, Brain of Cthulhu
Demon Scythe	Magic weapon, pierces through enemies	Underworld
Demonite Ore[2]	Used to craft Demonite Bar	Underground (rare), Eye of Cthulhu, Eater of Worlds
Depth Meter	Displays depth	Jungle, Underground, Underground Snow, Cavern
Diving Helmet	Extends underwater breathing	Ocean
Enchanted Sword	Rare melee weapon, fires projectile	Enchanted Sword Shrines
Eskimo Armor	4 Defense	Snow
Extractinator	Converts silt, slush and Desert Fossil	Snow, Underground Snow, Underground Desert, Gold Chests
Fish	Summons baby penguin pet	Underground Snow
Flipper	Allows swimming	Ocean
Flower Boots	Flowers grow when walking on grass	Underground Jungle
Flurry Boots	Allows super-fast running	Underground Snow
Flying Carpet	Allows floating for a few seconds	Desert
Gel	Ingredient in torch, Sticky Bomb, Lesser Healing Potion, etc.	Slimes
Gladiator Armor	7 Defense	Marble Caves
Glowstick	Light source, works underwater	Pots, chests, jellyfish
Guide Voodoo Doll	Summons Wall of Flesh when thrown in lava in Underworld	Underworld
Handgun	Gun, ingredient of Phoenix Blaster	Dungeon
Hellforge	Crafting station, like Furnace but can also smelt Hellstone	Underworld
Hook	Ingredient in grappling hook	Jungle, Underground, Underground Snow, Underground Jungle, Marble Caves, Cavern

1 Crimson worlds only   2 Corruption worlds only

ITEM	DESCRIPTION	SOURCE
Ice Blade	Melee weapon, shoots icy bolts	Underground Snow
Ice Boomerang	Boomerang, emits light	Underground Snow
Ice Skates	Increases control on ice, ice doesn't break when falling on it	Underground Snow
Javelin	Thrown weapon, can pierce through three enemies	Marble Caves
Jellyfish Necklace	Emits light underwater	Jellyfish
Jungle Rose	Vanity item	Jungle
Leaf Wand	Places Leaf Blocks in exchange for Wood	Living Trees
Life Crystal	Increases Health by 20, up to 400	Crystal Hearts
Living Loom	Crafting station, used to create Living Wood furniture	Living Trees
Living Wood Wand	Places Living Wood blocks in exchange for Wood	Living Trees
Lucky Horseshoe	Prevents fall damage	Floating Islands
Magic Lantern	Light pet makes treasure glow	Skeleton Merchant
Magic Mirror	Returns you home when used	Underground, Underground Jungle, Cavern
Magic Missile	Magic weapon, fires a bolt that can be controlled	Dungeon
Magma Stone	Sets enemies on fire when hit	Underworld
Metal Detector	Shows nearby precious metals	Cavern
Mining Armor	Increases mining speed, mining helmet emits light	Cavern
Muramasa	Auto-swing melee weapon, ingredient in Night's Edge	Dungeon
Nazar	Protects again curse, ingredient in Ankh Shield	Dungeon
Night Vision Helmet	2 Defense, enhances nearby lights	Granite Caves
Obsidian Rose	Reduces damage from lava	Underworld
Pharaoh's Clothes	Vanity items	Desert
Pink Gel	Used to create bouncy items	Forest, Underground, Cavern
Plumber's Hat	Vanity item	Underworld
Purple Mucos	Ingredient in purple dye	Ocean
Radar	Detects nearby enemies	Forest
Rally	Yo-yo weapon	Cavern
Robot Hat	Vanity item	Jungle, Underground Jungle
Rotten Chunk[2]	Used to craft leather, Battle Potion and worm food	Corruption
Sandstorm in a Bottle	Allows double-jump	Desert
Shadow Scale[2]	Ingredient in Shadow Armor, Nightmare Pickaxe and the Breaker	Eater of Worlds
Shark Fin	Ingredient in Hunter Potion, Water Walking Potion and Megashark	Ocean
Shiny Red Balloon	Increases jump height	Floating Islands
Sky Mill	Crafting station, used to craft sky-themed furniture	Floating Islands
Snowball Cannon	Ranged weapon, fires snowballs	Underground Snow
Snowball Launcher	Fires snowballs (doesn't cause damage)	Underground Snow
Spelunker Glowstick	Makes nearby treasure glow	Skeleton Merchant
Staff of Regrowth	Creates grass, harvests plants more effectively	Underground Jungle
Starfury	Melee weapon, fires a star projectile	Floating Islands
Stinger	Ingredient in Thorn Chakram, Blade of Grass, Amazon, etc.	Underground Jungle
Tally Counter	Displays monster kill count	Dungeon
Tattered Cloth	Used to craft Goblin Battle Standards, summons Goblin Army	Forest
Tissue Sample[1]	Used to craft Crimson Armor, Deatbringer Pickaxe, Flesh Grinder and the Meatball	Brain of Cthulhu
Umbrella Hat	Vanity item	Forest (during rain)
Valor	Yo-yo weapon	Dungeon
Vertebrae[1]	Ingredient in Bloody Spine and Battle Potion	Crimson
Viking Helmet	Vanity item	Underground Snow
Wand of Sparking	Magic weapon, fires piercing spark	Forest
Water Bolt	Magic weapon, pierces multiple enemies	Dungeon
Web Slinger	Grappling hook, can fire eight hooks simultaneously	Spider Nests
Whoopie Cushion	Novelty item, used to craft Fart in a Jar (allows double-jump)	Underground, Cavern
Wizard Hat	Increases magic damage	Cavern
Worm Tooth[2]	Used to craft Unholy Arrow and Thorns Potion	Corruption

1 Crimson worlds only   2 Corruption worlds only

HARDMODE TREASURE

	ITEM	DESCRIPTION	SOURCE
	Adhesive Bandage	Immune to bleeding, ingredient in Ankh Shield	Hardmode Dungeon, Jungle, Cavern
	Armor Polish	Immune to broken armor, ingredient in Ankh Shield	Hardmode Dungeon
	Black Belt	Change to dodge attacks	Hardmode Dungeon (Bone Lee)
	Blessed Apple	Summons Unicorn Mount	Hallow, Underground Hallow
	Blindfold	Immunity to darkness effect, ingredient in Ankh Shield	Corruption, Underground Corruption, Corrupted Desert
	Bone Feather	Used to craft Bone Wings	Hardmode Dungeon
	Chain Guillotines[2]	Chain melee weapon, auto-swings	Underground Corruption
	Clinger Staff[2]	Magic weapon, creates wall of Cursed Flame	Underground Corruption
	Crystal Vile Shard	Magic weapon, fires massive crystal spike	Underground Hallow
	Daedalus Stormbow	Bow, shoots arrows from the sky	Underground Hallow
	Dart Pistol[1]	Ranged weapon, shoots darts	Underground Crimson
	Dart Rifle[2]	Ranged weapon, shoots darts	Underground Corruption
	Ectoplasm	Used to craft Spectre Bars, Spectre Armor, Spectre tools and Spectre Wings	Hardmode Dungeon
	Fast Clock	Immune to slow effects, ingredient in Ankh Shield	Surface (night), Desert, Underground Desert, Hallow
	Fetid Baghnakhs[1]	Super-fast melee weapon	Underground Crimson
	Flesh Knuckles[1]	Increases Defense, monsters are more likely to target you	Underground Crimson
	Flying Knife	Melee weapon, throws reusable knife	Underground Hallow
	Illuminant Hook	Grappling hook, can fire three hooks at the same time	Underground Hallow
	Inferno Fork	Magic weapon, shoots fireball that sets enemies on fire	Hardmode Dungeon
	Keybrand	Melee weapon	Hardmode Dungeon
	Kraken	Yo-yo weapon	Hardmode Dungeon
	Life Drain[1]	Deals constant damage to nearby monsters and heals you	Underground Corruption
	Lizard Egg	Summons pet lizard	Lihzahrd Temple
	Magnet Sphere	Magic weapon, summons magnet sphere that attacks enemies	Hardmode Dungeon
	Meat Grinder[1]	Crafting station, turns Crimtane Blocks into Flesh Blocks	Underground Crimson
	Megaphone	Immune to silence effects, ingredient in Ankh Shield	Underground (water), Hallow, Corrupted Desert
	Moon Mask	Vanity item	Underground Corrupted Desert
	Paladin's Hammer	Boomerang weapon	Dungeon (Paladin)
	Paladin's Shield	Transfers 25% of damage from teammate to player (multiplayer)	Dungeon (Paladin)
	Piranha Gun	Ranged weapon, fires returning piranha	Dungeon (Jungle Chest)
	Pixie Dust	Ingredient in Greater Healing Potion, Holy Arrow, Fairy Bell, Fairy Wings, etc.	Hallow
	Putrid Scent[2]	Increases critical strike chance and makes monsters less likely to target you	Underground Corruption
	Rainbow Brick	Block that cycles through the colours of the rainbow	Hallow (rain)
	Rainbow Gun	Magic weapon, fires rainbow beam	Dungeon (Hallowed Chest)
	Rifle Scope	Increases view range of guns	Hardmode Dungeon (Skeleton Sniper)
	Rocket Launcher	Fires explosive rockets	Hardmode Dungeon (Skeleton Commando)
	Rod of Discord	Teleports you to the mouse pointer, causes damage if used repeatedly	Underground Hallow
	Scourge of the Corruptor[2]	Melee weapon, fires projectiles	Dungeon (Corruption Chest)
	Shadowbeam Staff	Magic weapon, fires beam that bounces off walls	Hardmode Dungeon
	Sniper Rifle	Ranged weapon with zoom ability and extreme long range	Hardmode Dungeon (Skeleton Sniper)
	Spectre Staff	Magic weapon, fires homing projectile	Hardmode Dungeon (Ragged Caster)
	SWAT Helmet	Vanity item	Hardmode Dungeon (Tactical Skeleton)
	Tabi	Dash ability	Hardmode Dungeon (Bone Lee)
	Tactical Shotgun	Ranged weapon, fires spread shots	Hardmode Dungeon (Tactical Skeleton)
	Tattered Bee Wing	Used to craft Bee Wings	Underground Jungle
	Tendon Hook[1]	Grappling hook, can fire three hooks at the same time	Underground Crimson
	Trifold Map	Immunity to confusion effects, ingredient in Ankh Shield	Blood Moon event, Hallowed Desert, Cavern
	Turtle Shell	Ingredient in Turtle Armor	Jungle, Underground Jungle
	Unicorn Horn	Used to craft Holy Arrow, Rainbow Rod and Super Mana Potion	Hallow
	Uzi	Gun, fires very fast	Jungle, Underground Jungle
	Vampire Knives[1]	Thrown melee weapon, returns some health with each hit	Dungeon (Crimson Chest)
	Vitamins	Protects against weakness, ingredient in Ankh Shield	Corruption, Underground Crimson
	Wisp in a Bottle	Summons Wisp light pet	Hardmode Dungeon
	Worm Hook[2]	Grappling hook, can fire three hooks at the same time	Underground Corruption

YOU MADE IT BACK! GOT ANYTHING INTERESTING TO SELL?

Now that you've seen all the wonders and terrors of this world, surely you understand why I can't settle down! Terraria is a vast place, filled with secrets and sights that can last you a lifetime!

But even your world is just one of the infinite possibilities that Terraria offers. Create a new world, and start exploring all over again. Or better yet, gather some friends and explore together! Just remember to come to me if you want a deal on all these precious artefacts you run across, all right?

Well, the open road is calling me. Cheerio, friend! See you somewhere interesting!

TERRARIA ONLINE

Check out these websites for help and inspiration for new adventures in the world of Terraria!

OFFICIAL WEBSITE
www.terraria.org

FACEBOOK PAGE
www.facebook.com/TerrariaOfficial

TWITTER ACCOUNT
www.twitter.com/Terraria_Logic

COMMUNITY FORUMS
forums.terraria.org

OFFICIAL TERRARIA WIKI
terraria.gamepedia.com

TERRARIA ON REDDIT*
www.reddit.com/r/Terraria

TERRARIA WIKIA*
terraria.wikia.com

* Websites not monitored by Re-Logic. Enter at your own risk!